Table of Contents

Welcome to "Financial Planning 101" - your comprehensive guide to building a strong financial foundation and achieving your financial goals. Whether you're just starting out on your financial journey or looking to fine-tune your existing financial plan, this guide will provide you with the knowledge and tools you need to succeed.

Financial planning can seem overwhelming at first, with so many options and decisions to make. But with the right guidance, anyone can learn how to manage their finances effectively and achieve financial security. In this book, we'll cover everything from creating a budget to managing debt, building an emergency fund, saving for retirement, and investing in the stock market.

We'll also address common financial pitfalls and offer tips for avoiding them, as well as practical strategies for staying motivated and on track with your financial goals. By the end of this book, you'll have a clear understanding of the fundamental principles of financial planning, and you'll be equipped with the tools and knowledge to make smart financial decisions that will set you up for a lifetime of financial success.

So whether you're looking to save for a down payment on a house, pay off student loans, or build a nest egg for retirement, "Financial Planning 101" is the perfect guide to help you achieve your financial goals and live the life you want.

SECTION 1: INTRODUCTION TO FINANCIAL PLANNING

DEFINITION OF FINANCIAL PLANNING

Financial planning refers to the process of setting and achieving personal or organizational financial goals by identifying financial objectives, gathering relevant financial information, and developing strategies to meet those objectives. It involves analyzing current financial status, creating a budget, setting long-term financial goals, and creating a plan to achieve those goals.

The primary purpose of financial planning is to ensure that an individual or organization can meet its financial obligations and achieve its financial objectives while also managing financial risks. This involves considering factors such as income, expenses, savings, investments, insurance, taxes, and retirement planning. By creating a comprehensive financial plan, individuals and organizations can make informed decisions about how to allocate their financial resources and make better financial decisions for the future.

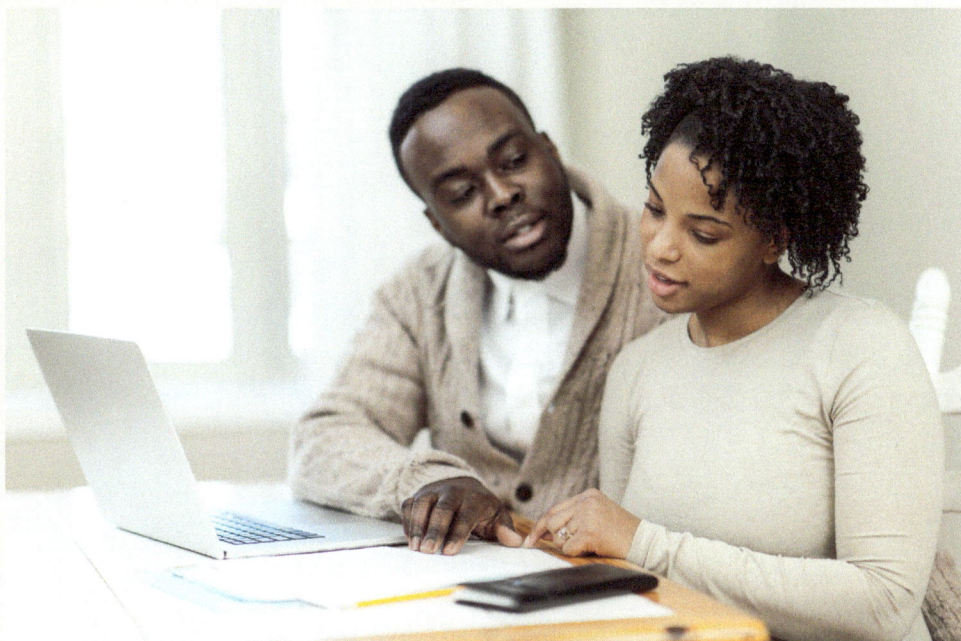

IMPORTANCE OF FINANCIAL PLANNING

Financial planning is important for several reasons:

Helps achieve financial goals: Financial planning provides a roadmap to achieve your financial goals. It helps you prioritize your financial objectives, create a budget, and develop a plan to achieve your goals. By following a financial plan, you can make better financial decisions and stay on track towards achieving your long-term financial goals.

Provides financial security: Financial planning helps you prepare for unexpected events such as job loss, illness, or other emergencies. By having an emergency fund, insurance coverage, and a plan for managing debt, you can minimize the financial impact of unexpected events and maintain financial stability.

Helps manage debt: Financial planning helps you manage debt by creating a plan to pay off debt, reducing interest payments, and avoiding unnecessary debt. By managing debt, you can improve your credit score, reduce financial stress, and increase your overall financial well-being.

Helps plan for retirement: Financial planning helps you plan for retirement by identifying your retirement goals, estimating your retirement expenses, and creating a retirement savings plan. By starting early and making regular contributions to retirement accounts, you can ensure a comfortable retirement.

Helps with tax planning: Financial planning helps you minimize taxes by taking advantage of tax deductions, credits, and tax-efficient investment strategies. By reducing taxes, you can increase your after-tax income and have more money to save and invest for the future.

Overall, financial planning is essential for achieving financial security, meeting financial goals, and building long-term wealth. It helps you make informed financial decisions, reduce financial stress, and improve your overall financial well-being.

KEY COMPONENTS OF A FINANCIAL PLAN

The key components of a financial plan can vary depending on individual circumstances and goals, but generally include the following:

Financial goals: A financial plan should begin with identifying your financial goals. These can include short-term goals like paying off debt or saving for a down payment on a house, as well as long-term goals like retirement savings or college education funding.

Budget: A budget is a critical component of a financial plan as it helps to track your income and expenses. Creating a budget involves estimating your monthly income, identifying your regular expenses (such as rent, utilities, and groceries), and setting aside money for savings and other goals.

Investment strategy: Developing an investment strategy involves identifying investment goals, assessing risk tolerance, and selecting suitable investment vehicles that align with your goals and risk profile. This includes choosing between stocks, bonds, mutual funds, exchange-traded funds (ETFs), and other investment options.

Retirement planning: Retirement planning is an important component of a financial plan as it helps to ensure you have enough money saved to cover living expenses in retirement. This includes estimating retirement expenses, creating a retirement savings plan, and determining the best retirement savings vehicles such as employer-sponsored retirement accounts, IRAs, or other investment accounts.

Estate planning: Estate planning involves creating a plan for the distribution of assets in the event of your death or incapacitation. This includes creating a will, setting up trusts, and designating beneficiaries for retirement accounts and insurance policies.

By including these key components in your financial plan, you can ensure that you are taking a comprehensive approach to achieving your financial goals and managing financial risks.

SECTION 2: ASSESSING YOUR FINANCIAL SITUATION
IDENTIFYING INCOME AND EXPENSES

Identifying income and expenses is an essential step in creating a budget and developing a financial plan. Here are some guidelines to help you identify your income and expenses:

Income: Start by identifying all sources of income, including your salary or wages, bonuses, tips, and other forms of compensation. You should also include any additional sources of income, such as rental income or investment income.

Fixed expenses: Fixed expenses are expenses that are the same amount each month, such as rent or mortgage payments, car payments, and insurance premiums. Make a list of all your fixed expenses and their monthly amounts.

Variable expenses: Variable expenses are expenses that change from month to month, such as groceries, dining out, entertainment, and utilities. Review your bank and credit card statements to determine your average monthly spending in these categories.

Periodic expenses: Periodic expenses are expenses that occur less frequently than monthly, such as car repairs, home maintenance, and vacations. Estimate the annual cost of these expenses and divide by 12 to determine the monthly cost.

Discretionary expenses: Discretionary expenses are non-essential expenses that are not required for basic living, such as hobbies, travel, and luxury items. Determine how much you typically spend on these expenses each month.

Once you have identified your income and expenses, you can use this information to create a budget and develop a financial plan. By tracking your income and expenses on an ongoing basis, you can adjust as needed to stay on track towards achieving your financial goals.

UNDERSTANDING DEBT AND CREDIT SCORES

Debt is an amount of money borrowed by an individual or an organization from a lender or a creditor with an agreement to pay back the borrowed amount along with interest. Debt can be in the form of a loan, credit card balance, mortgage, or any other form of borrowed funds. Managing debt is an essential part of financial planning as it can significantly impact your credit score and overall financial health.

A credit score is a number that represents an individual's creditworthiness based on their credit history. It is calculated by credit bureaus such as Equifax, Experian, and TransUnion based on factors such as payment history, amounts owed, length of credit history, types of credit used, and new credit applications. A credit score can range from 300 to 850, with a higher score indicating a lower risk of defaulting on debt.

Having a good credit score is important as it can impact your ability to borrow money, get approved for credit cards, and even rent an apartment or get a job. A high credit score can result in lower interest rates on loans and credit cards, which can save you money over time.

To maintain a good credit score, it's important to pay your bills on time, keep your credit utilization low, maintain a long credit history, and limit new credit applications. It's also important to review your credit report regularly to ensure that it is accurate and to address any errors that may negatively impact your credit score.

If you are struggling with debt or have a low credit score, there are steps you can take to improve your financial situation. This may include creating a budget to manage your expenses, consolidating debt with a low-interest loan or balance transfer credit card, or working with a credit counseling agency to develop a debt repayment plan. By taking steps to manage debt and improve your credit score, you can improve your overall financial health and achieve your financial goals.

ANALYZING YOUR NET WORTH

Analyzing your net worth is an important step in understanding your financial health and planning for your financial future. Net worth is the difference between your assets (what you own) and your liabilities (what you owe). It represents your overall financial position at a given point in time. To analyze your net worth, follow these steps:

Identify your assets: Make a list of all your assets, including cash, savings accounts, investments, retirement accounts, real estate, and personal property (such as cars, jewelry, and furniture). Estimate the current value of each asset.

Identify your liabilities: Make a list of all your liabilities, including mortgages, car loans, credit card balances, student loans, and any other debts you owe. Write down the outstanding balance on each liability.

Calculate your net worth: Subtract your liabilities from your assets to determine your net worth. If your assets exceed your liabilities, you have a positive net worth. If your liabilities exceed your assets, you have a negative net worth.

Analyze your net worth: Review your net worth and consider what it tells you about your overall financial health. If your net worth is positive, you have a good foundation for building wealth and achieving your financial goals. If your net worth is negative, it may indicate that you need to focus on paying off debt and building up your savings and investments.

By analyzing your net worth, you can identify areas where you may need to make changes to improve your financial situation. For example, if you have a negative net worth, you may need to focus on paying down debt and building up your emergency fund and retirement savings. If your net worth is positive, you may be able to focus on investing in assets that will help you achieve your long-term financial goals. Regularly analyzing your net worth can help you stay on track towards achieving your financial goals over time.

SECTION 3: SETTING FINANCIAL GOALS
TYPES OF FINANCIAL GOALS (SHORT-TERM, MID-TERM, LONG-TERM)

Financial goals can be categorized based on the time frame in which they need to be achieved. Here are the three main types of financial goals:

Short-term goals: Short-term financial goals are those that can be achieved within a year or less. Examples of short-term financial goals include building an emergency fund, paying off credit card debt, or saving for a vacation or a major purchase such as a car.

Mid-term goals: Mid-term financial goals are those that can be achieved within two to five years. Examples of mid-term financial goals include saving for a down payment on a home, paying for a child's education, or starting a business.

Long-term goals: Long-term financial goals are those that take more than five years to achieve. Examples of long-term financial goals include saving for retirement, paying off a mortgage, or building a substantial investment portfolio.

It's important to have a mix of short-term, mid-term, and long-term financial goals. Short-term goals can help you build momentum and stay motivated, while mid-term goals can help you plan for major life events and achieve bigger milestones. Long-term goals can help you focus on your financial future and ensure that you are prepared for retirement and other long-term needs.

When setting financial goals, it's important to make them specific, measurable, and realistic. This means setting a specific dollar amount and a target date for achieving each goal and creating a plan to achieve it. Regularly reviewing and adjusting your financial goals can also help you stay on track and achieve financial success over time.

S.M.A.R.T. GOAL SETTING

S.M.A.R.T. goal setting is a popular framework for setting goals that are specific, measurable, achievable, relevant, and time bound. The acronym stands for the following:

Specific: A specific goal is one that is clearly defined and unambiguous. It should answer the questions of who, what, when, where, and why. For example, instead of setting a goal to "save money," a specific goal would be "save $5,000 for a down payment on a house in the next 12 months."

Measurable: A measurable goal is one that can be tracked and quantified. It should include specific metrics that can be used to measure progress and determine when the goal has been achieved. For example, a measurable goal would be "save $416.67 per month for 12 months to reach a total of $5,000 for a down payment on a house."

Achievable: An achievable goal is one that is challenging but still realistic and attainable. It should be based on your current abilities and resources and consider any potential obstacles or challenges that may need to be overcome. For example, setting a goal to save $50,000 in one year on a $30,000 annual salary may not be achievable.

Relevant: A relevant goal is one that is aligned with your values, priorities, and overall vision for your life. It should be something that you are passionate about and motivated to achieve. For example, if your long-term goal is to own a home, a relevant short-term goal would be to save for a down payment.

Time-bound: A time-bound goal is one that has a specific deadline or target date for completion. It should be broken down into smaller milestones with specific dates to help you stay on track and measure progress. For example, a time-bound goal would be "save $416.67 per month for 12 months to reach a total of $5,000 for a down payment on a house by June 30th of next year."

By setting S.M.A.R.T. goals, you can increase your chances of success and make progress towards achieving your financial goals. It also helps you to stay focused and motivated throughout the process.

PRIORITIZING FINANCIAL GOALS

When it comes to prioritizing financial goals, it's important to consider both the urgency and importance of each goal. Here are some steps you can take to prioritize your financial goals:

Identify your financial goals: Make a list of all your financial goals, including short-term, mid-term, and long-term goals. This can include things like building an emergency fund, paying off debt, saving for retirement, and investing in the stock market.

Determine the urgency of each goal: Consider which goals are the most time-sensitive and require immediate attention. For example, if you have high-interest credit card debt, paying it off should be a top priority as it will save you money on interest charges in the long run.

Determine the importance of each goal: Consider which goals are most important to you and align with your values and long-term financial objectives. For example, saving for retirement may be a more important goal than taking a vacation, as it will have a greater impact on your financial well-being in the long run.

Rank your goals: Once you have determined the urgency and importance of each goal, rank them in order of priority. Start with the goals that are both urgent and important, then move on to those that are important but less urgent, and finally, those that are less important and less urgent.

Create a plan: Once you have prioritized your financial goals, create a plan to achieve them. This may involve setting specific targets for each goal, determining how much money you need to save each month, and identifying the steps you need to take to achieve each goal.

Remember, financial goals can change over time, so it's important to regularly review and adjust your priorities as needed. By prioritizing your financial goals, you can focus your resources and efforts on achieving the most important objectives first and work towards long-term financial success.

SECTION 4: CREATING A BUDGET
UNDERSTANDING THE IMPORTANCE OF A BUDGET

A budget is a financial plan that helps you track your income and expenses and manage your money effectively. Here are some reasons why having a budget is important:

Helps you track your spending: A budget helps you keep track of your income and expenses, which can help you identify areas where you may be overspending and where you can cut back.

Helps you save money: By tracking your expenses and identifying areas where you can cut back, you can save more money each month. This can help you achieve your financial goals, such as building an emergency fund, paying off debt, or saving for retirement.

Helps you avoid debt: By managing your expenses and living within your means, you can avoid accumulating debt or falling behind on bills. This can help you maintain a good credit score and avoid high interest rates and fees.

Helps you make better financial decisions: A budget provides a clear picture of your financial situation, which can help you make more informed decisions about how to spend your money. This can help you prioritize your spending and make choices that align with your financial goals.

Provides peace of mind: Knowing that you have a clear plan for managing your money can provide a sense of security and peace of mind. This can help you feel more in control of your finances and reduce stress and anxiety.

In summary, having a budget is an essential tool for managing your finances effectively and achieving your financial goals. It can help you track your spending, save money, avoid debt, make better financial decisions, and provide peace of mind.

STEPS TO CREATE A BUDGET

There are a few easy steps to creating a budget. Here are a few to get you started.

Determine your income: Start by calculating your total income for the month, including your salary, wages, tips, and any other sources of income.

Track your expenses: Keep track of all your expenses for a month, including fixed expenses such as rent or mortgage payments, utilities, insurance, and variable expenses such as groceries, entertainment, and clothing.

Categorize your expenses: Divide your expenses into categories, such as housing, transportation, food, entertainment, and savings. This will help you see where your money is going and identify areas where you can cut back.

Set financial goals: Determine your financial goals, such as paying off debt, building an emergency fund, or saving for a down payment on a house.

Allocate your income: Allocate your income to each expense category based on your financial goals and spending priorities. Make sure to leave some room for unexpected expenses and savings.

Review and adjust: Review your budget regularly to make sure you are staying on track and adjust as needed. You may need to cut back on certain expenses or increase your income to meet your financial goals.

Use a budgeting tool: Consider using a budgeting tool or app to help you track your expenses and stay on top of your budget. This can make it easier to see where your money is going and identify areas where you can save.

Remember, creating a budget is just the first step in managing your finances effectively. It's important to stick to your budget, track your expenses regularly, and adjust as needed to achieve your financial goals.

STRATEGIES FOR STICKING TO A BUDGET

Sticking to a budget can be challenging, but here are some strategies that can help:

Set realistic goals: When creating your budget, set realistic goals that you can achieve. This will make it easier to stick to your budget and stay motivated.

Keep Track of your expenses: Keep track of your expenses regularly to make sure you are staying within your budget. You can use a spreadsheet, an app, or a notebook to track your expenses.

Prioritize your spending: Identify the most important expenses and prioritize them in your budget. This can help you make sure that you are covering your essential expenses first.

Automate your savings: Consider setting up automatic transfers to your savings account to make sure you are saving regularly. This can help you build your emergency fund or save for a specific financial goal.

Use cash: Consider using cash for your discretionary spending, such as groceries or entertainment. This can help you stay within your budget and avoid overspending.

Limit your credit card use: Try to limit your credit card use to essential expenses only. This can help you avoid accumulating debt and overspending.

Find ways to save money: Look for ways to save money on your essential expenses, such as groceries, utilities, or transportation. This can help you free up more money for your financial goals.

Review and adjust regularly: Review your budget regularly and adjust as needed to make sure you are staying on track and making progress toward your financial goals.

By using these strategies and staying committed to your budget, you can achieve your financial goals and build a strong financial future.

SECTION 5: SAVING AND INVESTING
IMPORTANCE OF SAVING AND INVESTING

Saving and investing are both important for building long-term financial security. Here are some reasons why:

Emergencies: Saving money in an emergency fund can provide a safety net in case of unexpected expenses, such as medical bills, car repairs, or job loss.

Goals: Saving money can help you achieve your financial goals, such as buying a home, starting a business, or saving for retirement.

Compound interest: Investing your money can help it grow through compound interest. This means that the money you earn from your investments is reinvested, allowing you to earn interest on your interest over time.

Inflation: Investing your money can also help protect your savings from inflation, which can erode the purchasing power of your money over time.

Retirement: Investing in a retirement account, such as a 401(k) or IRA, can help you save for retirement and provide a steady stream of income in your later years.

Wealth building: Investing in stocks, mutual funds, or real estate can provide opportunities for long-term wealth building and financial independence.

By saving and investing wisely, you can build a strong financial foundation and achieve your long-term financial goals.

TYPES OF SAVINGS ACCOUNTS AND INVESTMENT OPTIONS

There are several types of savings accounts and investment options available. Here are some common examples:

Savings Accounts

Regular Savings Account: These accounts offer a low interest rate but are easily accessible and provide a safe place to store your money.

High-Yield Savings Account: These accounts offer higher interest rates than regular savings accounts but may require higher minimum balances or limit the number of withdrawals you can make.

Money Market Account: These accounts offer a higher interest rate than regular savings accounts and may require a higher minimum balance but allow more flexibility for withdrawals.

Investment Options

Stocks: Stocks represent ownership in a company and offer the potential for long-term growth, but also involve higher risk.

Bonds: Bonds are debt securities that offer a fixed rate of return and are generally considered a lower-risk investment option than stocks.

Mutual Funds: Mutual funds are professionally managed investment portfolios that pool money from many investors to purchase a diversified mix of stocks, bonds, and other assets.

Exchange-Traded Funds (ETFs): ETFs are like mutual funds, but trade like individual stocks on an exchange and often have lower fees.

Real Estate: Real estate investments can provide long-term growth and income through rental properties or real estate investment trusts (REITs). It's important to research and understand the risks and benefits of each type of savings account and investment option before making any decisions. Additionally, it's always a good idea to consult with a financial advisor to help guide your investment strategy.

STRATEGIES FOR BUILDING WEALTH OVER TIME

Building wealth over time requires a combination of smart saving, investing, and financial planning. Here are some strategies that can help:

Start early: The earlier you start saving and investing, the more time you must benefit from compound interest and long-term growth.

Set clear financial goals: Identify your financial goals and create a plan for achieving them, whether it's paying off debt, saving for a down payment on a home, or building a retirement nest egg.

Live below your means: To build wealth, you need to spend less than you earn. Create a budget and prioritize your spending to make sure you are living within your means.

Automate your savings: Set up automatic contributions to your savings and investment accounts to make sure you are consistently building your wealth over time.

Diversify your investments: Spread your investments across different asset classes, such as stocks, bonds, and real estate, to reduce risk and maximize returns.

Take advantage of tax-advantaged accounts: Use tax-advantaged accounts, such as 401(k)s, IRAs, and health savings accounts (HSAs), to save for retirement and reduce your tax burden.

Be patient: Building wealth takes time, so it's important to be patient and stay committed to your long-term financial goals.

By following these strategies and staying disciplined in your financial planning, you can build wealth over time and achieve financial security for yourself and your family.

SECTION 6: MANAGING DEBT
UNDERSTANDING DIFFERENT TYPES OF DEBT

There are several types of debt that people may encounter in their financial lives. Here are some common types:

Mortgage debt: This is a loan that is used to purchase a home. The home itself is used as collateral, meaning that the lender can seize the property if the borrower fails to make payments.

Student loan debt: This is money that is borrowed to pay for education expenses. Student loans can be provided by the government or by private lenders, and they typically have lower interest rates than other types of loans.

Credit card debt: This is debt that is incurred when a person uses a credit card to make purchases. Credit card debt can be particularly damaging because it often comes with high interest rates and fees.

Auto loan debt: This is a loan that is used to purchase a vehicle. The vehicle serves as collateral, so the lender can repossess it if the borrower fails to make payments.

Personal loan debt: This is a loan that is used for personal expenses, such as medical bills or home repairs. Personal loans can be secured or unsecured, and they typically have higher interest rates than other types of loans.

It's important to understand the different types of debt and their associated costs and risks when making financial decisions. Borrowing money can be useful in certain situations, but it's important to manage debt carefully to avoid getting into financial trouble.

STRATEGIES FOR PAYING OFF DEBT

Here are some strategies for paying off debt:

Create a budget: Start by creating a budget that tracks your income and expenses. This will help you identify areas where you can cut back on spending and free up money to put toward your debt.

Prioritize your debts: Identify which debts have the highest interest rates and prioritize paying them off first. This will help you save money on interest over time.

Make extra payments: Consider making extra payments on your debts whenever possible. This can help you pay off your debts faster and save money on interest.

Use the debt snowball method: This method involves paying off your smallest debts first and then moving on to your larger debts. By focusing on one debt at a time, you can build momentum and stay motivated.

Consider debt consolidation: If you have multiple high-interest debts, consolidating them into one loan with a lower interest rate can help you save money on interest and simplify your payments.

Negotiate with creditors: If you're struggling to make payments on your debts, consider reaching out to your creditors to see if they're willing to work with you. They may be willing to lower your interest rate, adjust your payment schedule, or offer other accommodations.

Seek professional help: If you're struggling to manage your debts on your own, consider reaching out to a financial advisor, credit counselor, or debt management company for help. They can provide guidance and support as you work to pay off your debts and get back on track financially.

By using these strategies and staying committed to paying off your debts, you can achieve financial freedom and build a strong financial future.

HOW TO AVOID DEBT IN THE FUTURE

Here are some tips to help you avoid debt in the future:

Create a budget: Start by creating a budget that tracks your income and expenses. This will help you identify areas where you can cut back on spending and save money.

Build an emergency fund: Having an emergency fund can help you avoid going into debt in case of unexpected expenses, such as medical bills or car repairs. Aim to save at least three to six months' worth of living expenses in an emergency fund.

Live within your means: Avoid overspending by living within your means. This means only spending money on things that you can afford and not relying on credit to make ends meet.

Avoid unnecessary debt: Avoid taking on unnecessary debt, such as high-interest credit card debt or loans for non-essential expenses.

Use credit responsibly: If you do use credit, use it responsibly by only charging what you can afford to pay off each month. This can help you avoid accumulating high levels of debt and damaging your credit score.

Seek financial education: Consider seeking out financial education to learn more about managing your money and avoiding debt. There are many resources available, including books, online courses, and financial advisors.

By using these tips and staying committed to responsible financial habits, you can avoid debt and build a strong financial future.

SECTION 7: RETIREMENT PLANNING
IMPORTANCE OF RETIREMENT PLANNING

Retirement planning is essential for several reasons:

Securing your financial future: Planning for retirement ensures that you have enough money to live on when you are no longer working. By starting early and consistently saving for retirement, you can build a solid financial foundation for your future.

Meeting your retirement goals: Retirement planning can help you define your retirement goals and determine the steps you need to take to achieve them. Whether you want to travel, buy a second home, or spend time with family, retirement planning can help you make those goals a reality.

Managing healthcare costs: As you get older, healthcare costs can become a significant expense. By planning for retirement, you can ensure that you have enough money set aside to cover these costs.

Taking advantage of tax benefits: Retirement planning can help you take advantage of tax benefits, such as contributions to tax-advantaged retirement accounts like IRAs and 401(k)s. These accounts can help reduce your tax burden and increase your retirement savings.

Minimizing the risk of outliving your savings: Without proper retirement planning, you run the risk of outliving your savings. By planning early and saving consistently, you can ensure that you have enough money to live on throughout your retirement years.

Overall, retirement planning is essential for securing your financial future, meeting your retirement goals, managing healthcare costs, taking advantage of tax benefits, and minimizing the risk of outliving your savings.

TYPES OF RETIREMENT ACCOUNTS

There are several types of retirement accounts available, including:

401(k): This is an employer-sponsored retirement plan that allows employees to contribute a portion of their salary on a pre-tax basis. Many employers offer matching contributions to help employees save for retirement.

Traditional IRA: This is an individual retirement account that allows you to make tax-deductible contributions and defer taxes until you withdraw the money in retirement.

Roth IRA: This is another type of individual retirement account that allows you to contribute after-tax dollars, and qualified withdrawals are tax-free.
SEP IRA: This is a Simplified Employee Pension plan that allows self-employed individuals and small business owners to contribute to a retirement account on behalf of themselves and their employees.
Simple IRA: This is a Savings Incentive Match Plan for Employees that is available to small businesses with 100 or fewer employees. It allows employees to contribute a portion of their salary on a pre-tax basis, and employers are required to make either a matching contribution or a non-elective contribution.
Pension plans: Pension plans are employer-sponsored retirement plans that provide a guaranteed income stream in retirement. These plans are becoming less common in the private sector, but they are still prevalent in some industries and government jobs.

It is essential to consider the tax implications, contribution limits, and withdrawal rules for each retirement account when deciding which one is best for you. A financial advisor can help you determine the best retirement account based on your specific needs and goals.

STRATEGIES FOR BUILDING A RETIREMENT NEST EGG
Here are some strategies for building a retirement nest egg:
Start saving early: The earlier you start saving for retirement, the more time your money must grow. Even if you can only save a small amount, it can add up over time.
Maximize contributions to retirement accounts: Contribute as much as you can to your employer-sponsored retirement plan, such as a 401(k), and individual retirement accounts (IRAs). Take advantage of any employer matching contributions and aim to contribute the maximum allowed by the IRS each year.

Diversify your investments: Invest in a mix of stocks, bonds, and other asset classes to help reduce risk and increase potential returns over the long term.

Consider a Roth IRA conversion: If you have a traditional IRA or 401(k), you may want to consider converting some or all of it to a Roth IRA. While you will have to pay taxes on the conversion, a Roth IRA allows tax-free withdrawals in retirement, which can be beneficial if you expect to be in a higher tax bracket in retirement.

Delay Social Security benefits: If possible, delay taking Social Security benefits until your full retirement age or beyond. This can increase your benefit amount and provide more income in retirement.

Keep your expenses in check: Live below your means and keep your expenses in check to free up more money for retirement savings.

Work with a financial advisor: A financial advisor can help you create a retirement plan, set goals, and develop a strategy to achieve them.

Remember, building a retirement nest egg takes time and discipline, but the earlier you start and the more consistent you are, the more likely you are to achieve your retirement goals.

SECTION 8: ESTATE PLANNING
UNDERSTANDING ESTATE PLANNING

Estate planning involves preparing a plan for the management and distribution of your assets after you pass away or become incapacitated. It can also involve planning for your healthcare and personal wishes if you become unable to make decisions for yourself.

Here are some important components of estate planning:
Will: A will be a legal document that outlines how you want your assets to be distributed after you pass away. It also allows you to name an executor to manage your estate and make sure your wishes are carried out.

Trusts: A trust is a legal arrangement that allows you to transfer assets to a trustee who will manage them on behalf of your beneficiaries. Trusts can provide more control over how and when assets are distributed and can also help minimize taxes.

Power of attorney: A power of attorney is a legal document that allows you to appoint someone to make financial or healthcare decisions on your behalf if you become incapacitated.

Health care directives: Health care directives allow you to specify your medical wishes if you are unable to make decisions for yourself. This can include specifying the types of medical treatments you want or don't want, as well as appointing a healthcare agent to make decisions on your behalf.

Beneficiary designations: Make sure that your beneficiary designations are up to date on all your accounts, such as retirement accounts, life insurance policies, and bank accounts. These designations will determine who receives your assets upon your death, regardless of what your will or trust says.

Estate planning is an important process that can provide peace of mind and ensure that your wishes are carried out after you pass away or become incapacitated. It's important to work with a qualified estate planning attorney and financial advisor to create a plan that meets your unique needs and goals.

IMPORTANCE OF ESTATE PLANNING

Estate planning is important for several reasons:

Ensures your assets are distributed according to your wishes: Estate planning allows you to specify how you want your assets to be distributed after you pass away. This can help avoid conflicts and disputes among family members and ensure that your assets are distributed according to your wishes.

Protects your loved ones: Estate planning can help protect your loved ones in the event of your incapacity or death. A power of attorney and health care directive can ensure that someone you trust is able to make decisions on your behalf if you are unable to do so. A will or trust can ensure that your assets are distributed to your beneficiaries according to your wishes, which can help provide for your loved ones after you are gone.

Reduces taxes: Proper estate planning can help minimize estate and gift taxes, which can save your beneficiaries money in the long run.

Provides for your business: If you own a business, estate planning can help ensure that your business continues to operate smoothly after you pass away or become incapacitated. This can help protect your employees and provide for your family.

Gives you peace of mind: Creating an estate plan can give you peace of mind knowing that your affairs are in order and your loved ones will be taken care of according to your wishes.

Overall, estate planning is an important process that can help provide for your loved ones, protect your assets, and give you peace of mind. It's important to work with a qualified estate planning attorney and financial advisor to create a plan that meets your unique needs and goals.

KEY COMPONENTS OF AN ESTATE PLAN

An estate plan typically includes several key components:

Will or Trust: A will, or trust is a legal document that outlines how your assets will be distributed after you pass away. It can also name an executor or trustee to manage your affairs, and guardians for minor children.

Power of Attorney: A power of attorney is a legal document that designates someone to manage your financial and legal affairs if you become incapacitated.

Health Care Directive: A health care directive, also known as a living, will or advance directive, outlines your wishes for medical treatment if you become unable to make decisions for yourself.

Beneficiary Designations: Many assets, such as retirement accounts and life insurance policies, allow you to name beneficiaries. Make sure your beneficiary designations are up to date and consistent with your estate plan.

Letter of Instruction: A letter of instruction is a non-binding document that outlines your wishes for funeral arrangements, distribution of personal property, and other important details.

Business Succession Plan: If you own a business, you may need a plan in place to ensure its continued operation after you pass away.

Estate Tax Planning: If your estate is large enough to be subject to estate taxes, you may need to implement strategies to minimize your tax liability.

Overall, an estate plan should be tailored to your unique needs and goals. It's important to work with a qualified estate planning attorney and financial advisor to create a plan that meets your specific needs.

Congratulations! You've made it to the end of this financial planning 101 guide. By following the steps outlined in this book, you should now have a good foundation for managing your money and achieving your financial goals.

Remember that financial planning is an ongoing process. It's important to regularly review and adjust your budget, savings plan, and investments as your circumstances and goals change.

Here are some additional tips to keep in mind:

- Be mindful of your spending and avoid unnecessary purchases.
- Build an emergency fund to cover unexpected expenses.
- Pay off high-interest debt before investing.
- Diversify your investments to minimize risk.
- Stay informed about changes in tax laws and other financial regulations that could affect your finances.

By taking control of your finances and making smart decisions, you can achieve financial stability and reach your long-term goals. Best of luck on your financial journey!